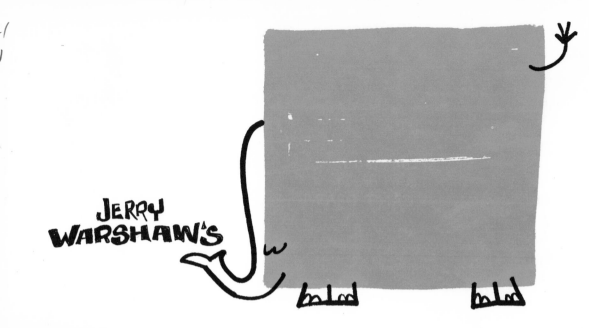

Jerry Warshaw's

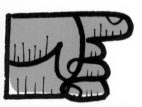 ## The I-CAN'T-DRAW BOOK

photography by Dick MASEK

ALBERT WHITMAN & Company
CHICAGO

I can't draw!
I can't draw!
I CAN'T DRAW!

Balderdash!

This book will prove that anyone can draw
by using simple shapes and lines.

I call these "picture starters"
because once started, you'll find
that drawing can be FUN

ISBN 0-8075-3502-8; L.C. CARD NUMBER 73-165824. © 1971 BY JERRY WARSHAW. ALL RIGHTS RESERVED
PUBLISHED SIMULTANEOUSLY IN CANADA BY GEORGE J. McLEOD, LIMITED, TORONTO. PRINTED IN U.S.A.

KEEP MATERIALS SIMPLE

Big felt-tip pen,
chalk or crayon
Paper to draw on
(almost any kind will do)
Things to help you draw
circles and lines—
a jar lid, a drinking glass,
small boxes—anything handy

Make big bold strokes

THE KEY TO
BEING AN
ARTIST
IS
SIMPLY—

OBSERVATION

Learn to look
at people and things,
and you'll find your mind
will begin to take things in
the way a sponge does.

For instance, take your neighborhood—

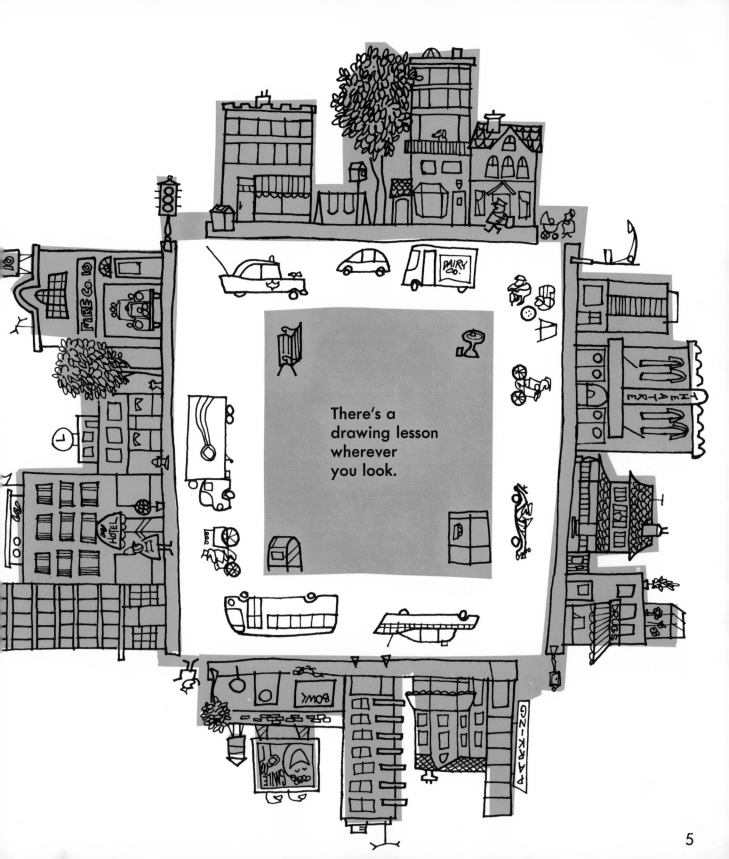

There's a
drawing lesson
wherever
you look.

FIRE Co. 10

HOTEL

DAIRY Co.

BOWL

SMILE

PARKING

5

Become a:
PEOPLE-WATCHER
BIRD-WATCHER
ANIMAL-WATCHER
EVERYTHING-WATCHER

The best place to be an everything-watcher is at the zoo.
People and birds and animals are all there.

REMEMBER
We want to draw
the impression,
or caricature,
of what we see.

Things have
SHAPES
and . . .

7

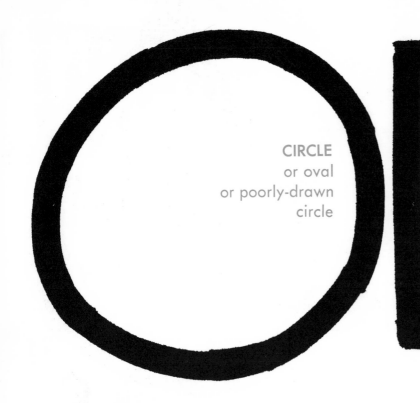

CIRCLE
or oval
or poorly-drawn
circle

SQUARE
or **RECTANGLE**
or poorly-drawn square
or what have you

These shapes
are all
that's needed
to start
you
drawing
everything
around you.

the BASIC SHAPES
AND THINGS
as picture starters

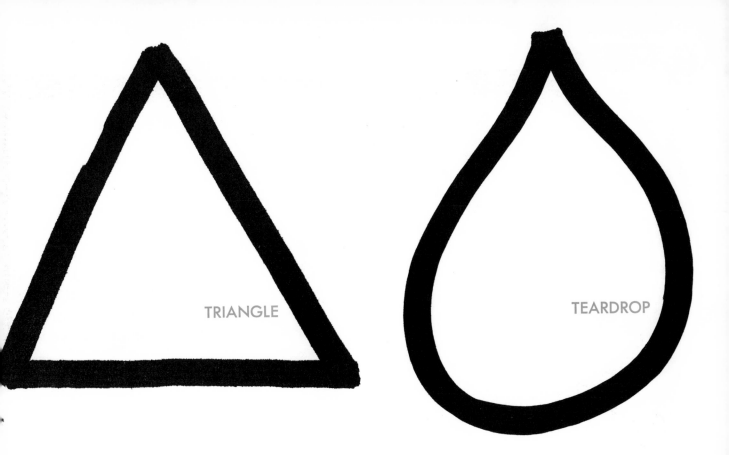

TRIANGLE

TEARDROP

BUNCH OF BANANAS

Assortment of **LINES**
straight, squiggly
and otherwise

W (my favorite letter)

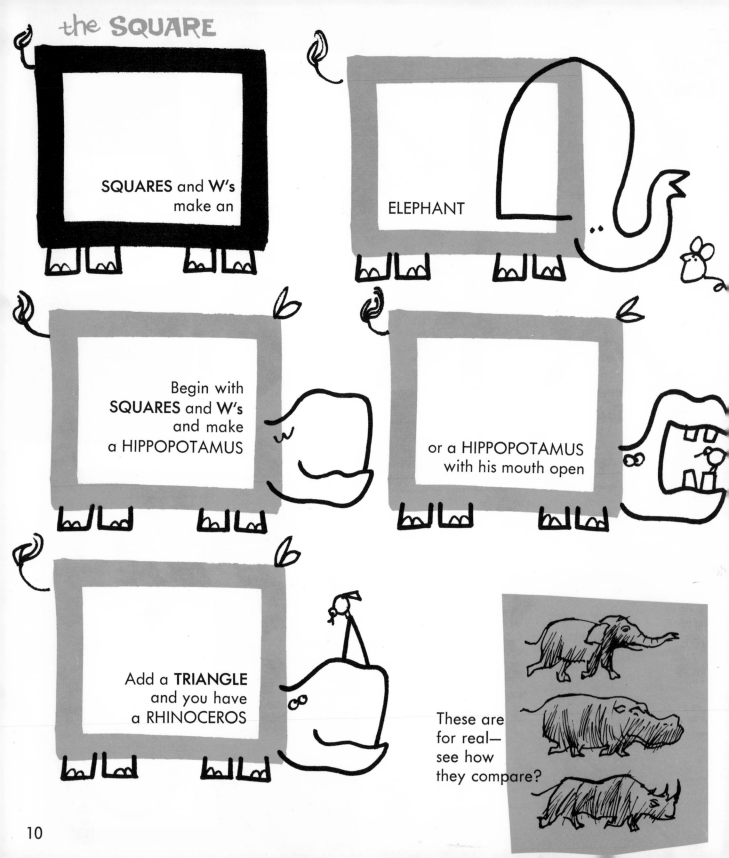

SQUARES and **W's** make an

ELEPHANT

Begin with **SQUARES** and **W's** and make a HIPPOPOTAMUS

or a HIPPOPOTAMUS with his mouth open

Add a **TRIANGLE** and you have a RHINOCEROS

These are for real— see how they compare?

the TEAR-DROP

BIRD
looking up
and
PROUD
BIRD

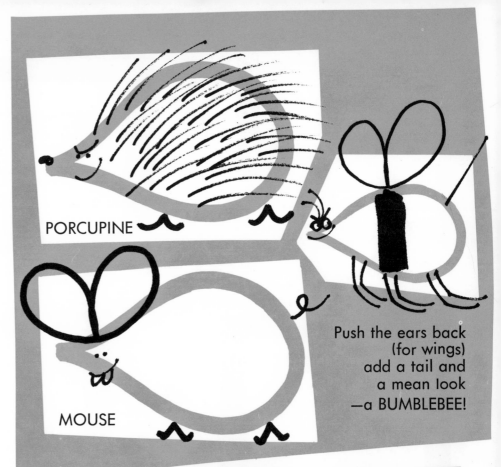

PORCUPINE

MOUSE

Push the ears back
(for wings)
add a tail and
a mean look
—a BUMBLEBEE!

Turn the
TEARDROP
over and cut off
the bottom and
you have
a PENGUIN

TEARDROP with
point side up
and the top
cut off, and you
have an OWL

PENGUIN

OWL

11

CIRCLE TRIANGLE

1 Begin with a CIRCLE and TRIANGLE,

2 add three little triangles,

3 two ovals, a W, and a wavy line

4 Put in lines for stripes, whiskers and eyes

Little CIRCLE and big TRIANGLE

This cat had its back to you but turned its head around when it heard you.

Mother cat

If you feel brave, turn the lion around, add a W for feet

Now turn the nose and you have a—?

But make the lion's back feet pigeon-toed so he can't catch you!

CIRCLE

TRIANGLE

IMPORTANT: ← When drawing people, be sure to move the ears down.

12

Big CIRCLE and
little TRIANGLE

Round the ears
and lengthen the nose

No stripes, but add tail and mane

Kitten

Make him mean—the lion's King of the Jungle

Draw the CIRCLE and TRIANGLE like this:

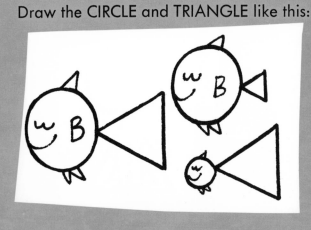

ACTION!

Animal walking

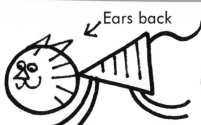

Ears back

Animal running

Animal racing

13

The best way to learn about expressions
is to look into a mirror as you think
about things—happy—sad—afraid—surprised

Watch people around you and see how their faces
show their feelings

EXPRESSIONS

People have expressions

so do animals

Now take your felt-tip marker
and a jar lid
or whatever you have that's round
and make a couple of
big circles.

Add some little
circles you draw
and a triangle—

Now tell yourself a story
and finish the face on your
paper.

Remember:
Drawing a picture
is like acting
in a play.
If you feel the expression
you are trying to draw,
it will almost
draw itself.

So—make faces
while you are
making faces . . . .

FRONT VIEW

SIDE VIEW

15

Let's see if we
can make up
a story about why
these faces are:

Man

Woman

Boy

Girl

Man with moustache

Animal

MEAN
just plain mean

MEAN
with a plan

UPSET

UNHAPPY

SCARED

HAPPY

VERY HAPPY

MAD

TIRED

STERN

The next step in drawing faces is the three-quarter view:

Happy   Sad   Mad   Thoughtful   Tired   and back view: Frightened

16

Take the alphabet and see what you can come up with, turning the letters, and adding to them. My own favorite letter is W. What's yours? Here I'm going to see how many alphabet expressions I can make.

See what you can do!

Picture people are people who live
in the world of "picture starters."
They are really our old buddies,
the CIRCLE, SQUARE, TRIANGLE, TEARDROP
and assorted lines and bananas all dressed up

Picture People

PICTURE PEOPLE

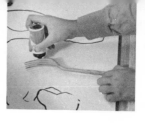

Take your felt-tip marker and trace around whatever you have

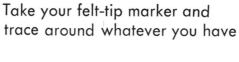

Picture
Starters

JAR LIDS
SPOONS, FORKS
TABLE KNIVES
TOY FURNITURE
LITTLE BOXES
SCISSORS
TOYS
LOCK

KITCHEN UTENSILS
   if Mother says OK

TOOLS
   if Dad says OK

   See what
   these shapes
   suggest to
   YOU

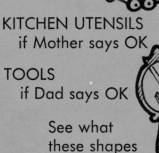

SAND SHOVEL

DOLL CHAIR

Riding an angry elephant can be unsettling—but it's better than getting squirted in the face.

SPOON

When the cannon went off, the man inside was happier than the man outside. Why?

PADLOCK

The engineer banged his bell— handcar get out of the way!

HAMMER

21

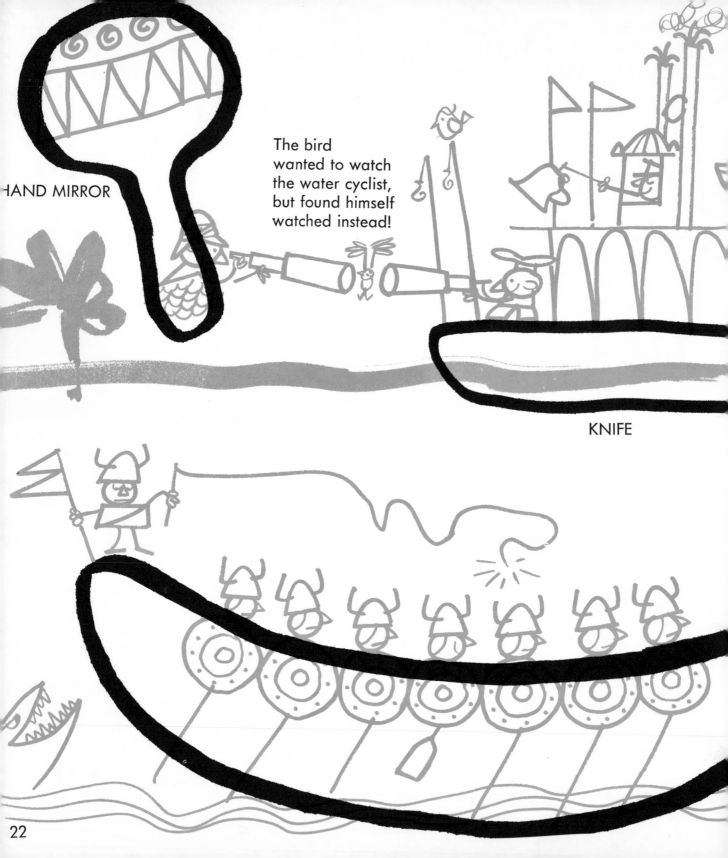

HAND MIRROR

The bird
wanted to watch
the water cyclist,
but found himself
watched instead!

KNIFE

The water cyclist had a hard time keeping his eye on the ship because of the smoke—But it was better than being at the other end, I think.

LOLLIPOP

BANANA

A smiling Viking doesn't let a grrrrring sea monster scare him—or does he?

GRRRRRRRRRRRRRRR

SCISSORS

**Getting started
another way . . .**

Your hand is probably
the easiest and most fun
to trace.
It makes a great
picture starter.

THUMB and FOREFINGER

TIPS of FINGERS

FINGER TIPS
upside down

TIPS of FINGERS and THUM

FIRST and SECOND FINGERS

FIRST and SECOND FINGERS

MIDDLE FINGERS

THUMB bent
side view

FINGER, side view

25

Take paper, crumple it up, then hold it in front of a lamp so that it casts a shadow. Trace around the shadow and let your imagination run wild.

Balance
can
make
all
the
difference
when
you
want to
be a
strongman

Sometimes
it's hard
to remember
it's birds who
are afraid
of cats!

Puttering around

Climbing "just because it's there" doesn't seem to be enough reason after all

Nothing here! What do you think I might have made?

Not our kind of landing!

A surprised dog wears a surprised look

Too much bait and too little boat

The "Simple Drawing Zoo" will be your own impressions of real animals.
So before we start, let's see what the animals really look like.

The SIMPLE DRAWING ZOO

Think about what makes
a giraffe a giraffe
or a kangaroo a kangaroo . . .

the SIMPLE DRAWING ZOO

Put together CIRCLES, TRIANGLES, SQUARES, LINES, TEARDROPS, W's, BANANAS and all the things you've tried and have fun.

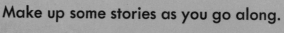

Make up some stories as you go along.

A camel can go for eight days without water, but maybe he can't count. What then?

The rabbit isn't worried. He has four rabbit's feet for luck and he can hippity-hope.

30

The nicest thing about having a giraffe and a beaver for pets is letting them share the same tree.

Never get in the way of a hurrying kangaroo with a passenger.

The cow misunderstood—she thought someone said kicked cream, not whipped cream.

The bird told the pig to try oinkment for his sore throat.

Here's author-artist Jerry Warshaw
with his daughter Elizabeth
and some funny pictures
they drew while making this book.
Did they have a good time?
They certainly did,
and so will you, now that
you say "I CAN DRAW!"